CW00410541

# JUST ASKING

**Bert Flitcroft**

**Just Asking**



First Edition 2021



Published by Dempsey & Windle
15 Rosetrees
Guildford
Surrey
GU1 2HS
UK
01483 571164
dempseyandwindle.com

British Library Cataloguing-in-Publication Data

A catalogue record for this book is available from the British Library

ISBN: 978-1-013329-35-8

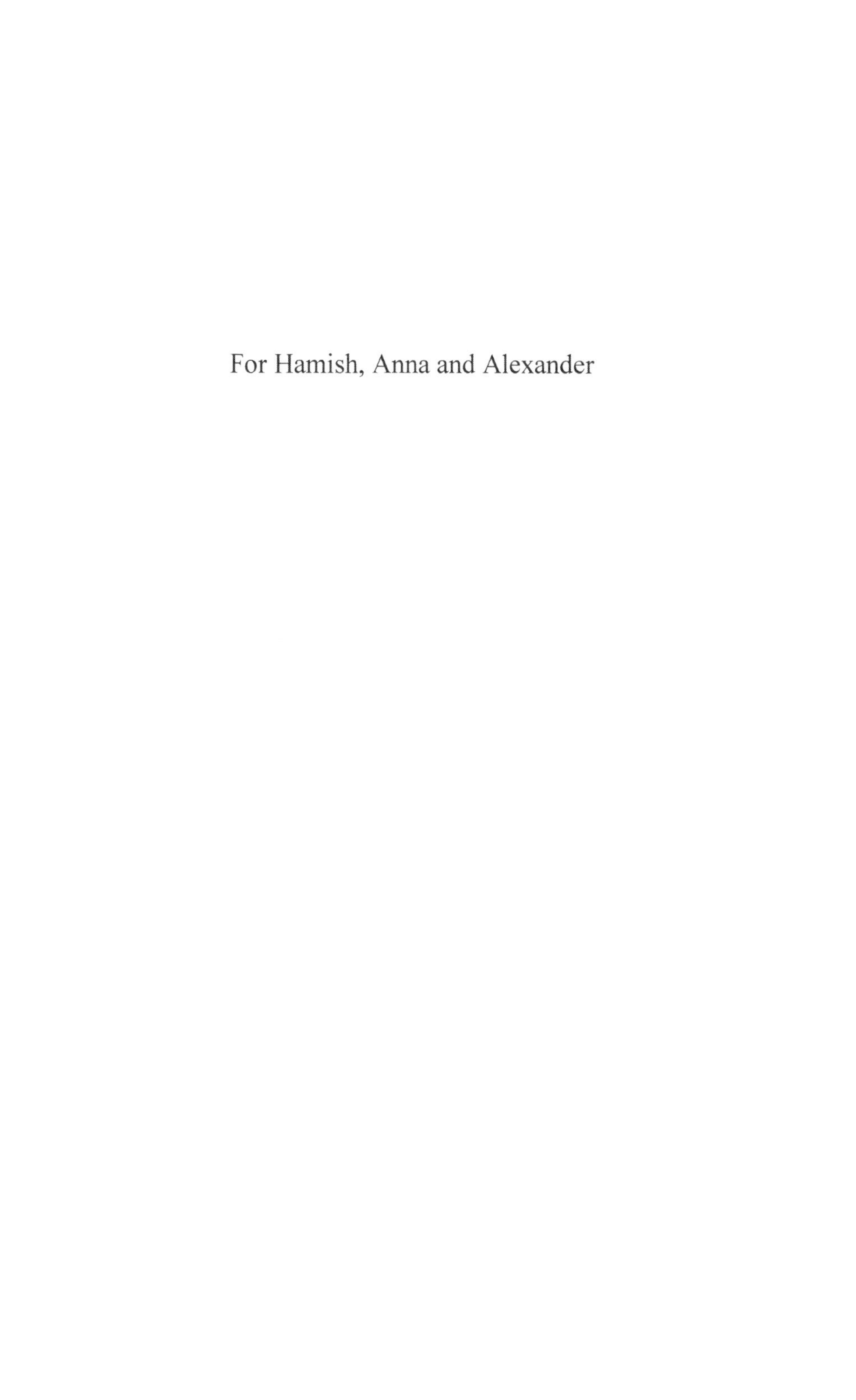

For Hamish, Anna and Alexander

**Contents**

## It's grim....

Have you been, to The North?
They say, up there they have an ugly angel,
a rust-coloured, furnace-welded crucifix
with the wingspan of a stadium,
a man of steel holding up the sky
around the fraying edges of the city.

Like Lear, it seems, he is a challenge
to every storm and bolt of lightning.
And he casts a shadow on our conscience,
yours and mine, they say, like a sin.

Sad, really. I've seen a photograph.
They say it is deliberately a shocking sight.
Like celebrating grime, I'd say.
You cannot see love in his eyes,
he has no eyes.
Beauty? It can't be in his smile,
he has no mouth to smile.

No fallen angel this, they say.
Stand at his feet, they say. Look up
at his thick-ribbed pride,
his barrel chest, the bulging calves,
that muscle out their industrial presence,
as if he is watching over them. As if
he is bolted into the bedrock of their being.
It's how they stand up in the world,
apparently.

## Claymills Pumping Station

A place, once named, needs a reason to grow.
Here it was gypsum and pale ale, fermented
into dense paragraphs of terraces and closets.
Once grown, think ugliness. Think effluence,
and sewage, typhoid and stink. Think Human.

Inside this temple, think… Grace, the beauty
of beam engines weighing in at thirteen tonnes,
rocking smoothly as a cradle and in harmony,
nodding like gentle giants at ease with their work,
their cast-iron skins spannered with precision.

Think elegance. Listen, to the steady pulse
of steam, the silk-smooth motion of their limbs.
Think quiet. There is a lullaby of engines here,
a symphony of nuts and bolts, a score of pipes
and stops, of wood and brass, played pianissimo.

Listen, to the language of wibblers and agitators,
Jubilee tubs and governors and Lancashire boilers;
the voices of stokers and strikers and welders,
layers and fitters, slakers and scalers; whole families
who were born and engineered, married and died here.

Think of the Pountains, the Scattergoods and Beadmans
painting bricks white around the doors during blackouts.
All gone. Only the stair rails of their cottages remain,
restored as safety barriers inside the boiler room.
The last remains. Nice touch that.

The Victorians knew a thing or two,
imagined what they did not know,
and understood the need for reciprocation.
Give me such machines, this elegance of motion.
Nod on, you beauties, into the future.
Nourish us.

## Beautiful?

They are still with you, the filthy rich
who love to hunt or trap or blast
their victims, then scour each soft skin,
slickly disembowel it and stuff
with coarse-fibred wool, hemp and arsenic,
as if to promise eternal life.

They thought us beautiful, and we were,
but mounted us like trophies on walls,
perched us beneath glass domes,
displayed our plump colourful breasts
and plumage on their mantles.
They thought we were stone dead.

Now we whisper in dark pain and wait
for first light, while the stink
of arsenical soap and turps lingers
in our nostrils. We cannot stretch
or reach or bend our will.
Our wire bones and sinews are too stiff
to turn and face, to see with glass eyes
each other's withered legs and feet,
the fans of our dirty, desiccated wings.

And these proud mahogany grandfathers
in their best and bees-waxed coats
as if on sentry duty, locked tight
with their deadweight pendulums,
they too have passed into the silence.
We sang in a glorious monstrous age.

*Written in a museum's 'Victorian Room'*

## We are such stuff

It is bustling in The Fat Cat Cafe.
Chairs are jostling for elbow room, wrestling
with legs and space and awkward prams,
and the bubbling chatter is a froth you could surf.
A man, his elbows on the table, is reading
'A History of Frogs in Transylvania',
raising his eyes now and then to re-locate himself.
In a crowd it is the single ones you notice,
those who want to be alone with others around them.

He could be a Naturalist in love with anurans,
a visiting Professor of Romanian Literature,
or a worker from the car wash up the road
escaping, like a free radical feeding on his dreams.
We are all somewhere else, most of the time.
Either way he does not seem to be lonely or lost.
He is focused, crouching by a green pond,
blindly reaching out to levitate a skinny cappuccino
to his lips, to entice a tiny fire-bellied toad.

## To my friends: just asking…

Some days I have nothing new to say
of consequence. No opinion about the rain,
no forthright view about the latest scandal
or the smell of crusty bread.
But should something startling happen:
an angel threaten to descend
or a best friend lost, or an old love found,
these are surely pearls worth diving for.

We have swum in the same sea for years,
so why, when the water feels deep
do you lapse into awkward silence,
close up your hearts and seal them
as tight as oyster shells?
Why the need to keep a cancer secret,
or treat a shortage of sex as a shame
as if it were a sweet grape
withered to an unspeakable raisin?
Or admit to the heat of unrequited love
that has scorched the heart of all of us?
As if these things were a moral failing
or a sign of weakness.

My life is full of conversations I do not have.
This is a matter of soul.
Some days I might as well be up a mountain
shouting into the ice-blue emptiness,
or in the supermarket buying beer and oranges.

## Buying mushrooms at Sainsbury's

In darkness some creatures give off light,
like a gift, a little homage to the sun,
but a mushroom in the dark is forced
to send out a trace of sweet scent, a signal
like a single pulse across the universe
that whispers, *I'm here. Am I alone?*
*Is there anyone there?*
In the end we all howl at the moon,
then find other ways of signaling.
I like bright red socks and blue shoes.
This slow cashier at the supermarket till
is sending out the scent of her livid lipstick.

## Targets

I pass him every morning on my way
to the office, see his moon face
out of the corner of my eye.
Most days I envy him his outdoor life,
out in in all weathers enjoying the fresh air,
the sunshine and showers, a view of the hills.
Enjoying the colours and shapes of traffic,
the steady stream of advertisements.
But mostly, just getting on with his job,
having a sense of purpose.

Today I have pulled over to say hello.
Something is amiss, the way his arms
are flung out wide as if in supplication,
his head lolling to one side. He looks stiff
with cold and the biting wind, tired
of the constant smell of slurry and damp soil.
As if he's had enough.

I know how he feels.
Just one job to do, but the relentless effort
like a salesman who can’t make his targets.
Being rooted and vulnerable, as helpless
as a soldier on the battlefield without a gun.
And that feeling of being a failure,
being ignored by the damn rooks and crows.

## Instinct

I am not a psychopath, a sadist or a butcher,
but when indoors I kill. I murder spiders.
If they are small I squash them in a tissue
or flush them down into the void of the plug.
If they are large I will trap them in a jar,
leave them to die neglected on a windowsill.

I cannot bring myself to stamp on them
like an assassin, as if my feet were clubs.
I do it gently, remotely, to create vicarious death.
If I have to I wear shoes; flesh is full of feeling
and socks allow too much texture on the skin.
I want them dead, that's all I know.

I would not dream of murdering a butterfly.
They are outdoors and not invasive.
I stop to admire them when they rest:
the delicacy of their white wings,
the red-brown beauty of an admiral,
the blue of a peacock like an iris,
although in flight they are elusive, settling
and shifting and weaving like politicians.
Like lies, their eyes a beautiful deceit.

## Boundaries

Boxing Day. The market square heaving
with gilets and wax jackets,
with the wellie-wearing country set
packed into this damp theatrical place
with its cast of hunting pink and stirrups.
They have come to share the animal ritual,
to savour the hint and whiff of fox,
to acknowledge deep roots.

They have come to tug their forelocks,
to doff their caps at the toffs
with their inherited certainty, their stash of land
grand enough to pay for packs of dogs.
They raise their eyes as if in homage, gawping
at the great and the good, the jodhpured gods
astride their Olympian mounts
looking down on this puny world.

One of the riders smiles at a face
in the crowd, then winks at The Master
who stands in his stirrups to adjust himself.
The muscular rump of his hunter stands stock-still,
the solid bulk of its haunches relaxed,
its cold, brown eyes as hard as stones.
It will brook no argument,
waiting for the madcap dash across the fields,
the ecstasy of sailing over hedges and fences,
leaping boundaries as if they were not there.

The pack, milling about with their busy tails,
know only the instinct to chase a quarry down.
They are impatient for the horn's shrill clarion,
the trot along the road before the hectic chase
through woods, over streams and ditches,
through all those manicured gardens.

## I love my garden. I could sit in it all day

admiring those pink flowers on the what-do-you-call-it
and the purple stuff in the pots on the patio.

In spring I like the yellow flowers that look like
sad trumpets drooping on tall green pencils

and those purple grape thing-a-my-jigs
sprouting out between the rockery weeds.

I adore the summer soapy smell of a red rose
and I'm quite partial to the uji-my-flip by the big tree,

as well as that round bushy thing like a bad haircut
destroying the neat straight lines of the lawn

The pretty white blossom stuff on that old tree is nice,
by the bottom fence where the field sweeps up.

I love the constant flutter of those little brown birds,
the kind of tits that flit in and out of the thick hedge,

and the chatter of crows, and the joyful song of the two
black birds whose territory cuts my mossy lawn in half.

I can tell my carnivores from my herbivores, too.
I'm happy to watch the joy of the tug for a juicy worm,

although I can't quite make up my mind about that
copper shrub thing in the corner which attracts the wasps,

as well as the what's-its-name beside the shed
where those fat birds sit silhouetted like vultures.

**Birds**

I’ve decided, I must try to love birds,
as my wife does. Eyes skyward she searches
for them, ears finely tuned to songs
and warbles, pointing out on our walks
the wheel of a buzzard over distant trees,
a robin in a winter hedgerow by the still canal,
different families of sparrows in the garden.

Yesterday, I watched nervous long-tailed tits
like acrobats sharing the hanging peanuts,
the bullying magpie in his glossy bib-and-tucker
who’s mastered the art of clinging sideways on
like a stuntman, picking at a suet ball.
And a pair of plump, pink-breasted wood pigeons
waddling down to hoover up the scatterings.

I know there's beauty in Nature, in a flash
of blue or the white glide of a barn owl.
But love is proving beyond me.
I’m left with a question which may be in there
waiting to hatch, or may never be answered:
can you force a feeling into being,
just by willing it?

## Blackbird

Sometimes, when the local teenagers
are skateboarding or loitering elsewhere
I sit on the bench across the road
seeing my front door as the postman sees it,
as the cat on the corner must.

Just now a blackbird is silhouetted on the eaves,
the thrill of his notes charging the fading light.
Though not a darkling thrush flinging out his soul,
and it is summertime not winter, that poem,
the suddenness and joy of it, is here.

The blackbird is indifferent to the yellow rumble
of the late bus that stops and then accelerates away.
He is busy summoning a distant mate perhaps
or throwing out a warning, guarding
his patch as more than darkness descends.

The evening's sieve of stars is brightening.
I should go in and turn on the table lamp,
but not just yet, while he is in full voice
and I am held in the palm of his song, the spell
of his silver notes defying the fading light.

## Walking to the Co-op. 7.00am

I'm up early and on a mission.
Frost is comatose on the drive
but melting on the lawn,
and glimmering
as if the air has coughed up
heavy droplets of The Virus.
I fear they may be lurking
in the air as well, like warnings.
And yet the sky is blue with promise
and a bumble bee has settled
on the spikes of grass, oblivious.
Thrush and blackbird, tree-topped,
are harvesting the warmth of early sun,
their notes springing out through
molecules of pure untainted air.

The village is still asleep.
How good it feels, strolling early
as if released for good behaviour,
like the first day out of hospital
when the joy of life is heightened.
And yet that distant grumble of tyres
is rolling angels and key workers
to their heroic jobs, lorries replete
with Weetabix and wine
and Pink Lady apples
rumbling to their allotted slots.

Soon, police cars will be racing
to disperse Orwellian labourers
gathering in green spaces, on beaches;

lost souls who are refusing to listen.
Even the line of black bins here
appear to be loitering with intent.

At no. 58 the Magnolia is stretching
itself awake, healthy in its isolation,
but just beyond, the bungalows,
with their pale unopened curtains,
look hunkered down for the duration.
I wonder if they are slumbering inside,
dreaming of wide open prairies,
or simply lying dead to the world.
Much better to be up and ambling,
knowing there will be skimmed milk
on the stacked shelf when I arrive.

Just now my shadow, long in the early sun,
is zigging up and zagging over
the kerbstone as if he's flinching
and wants to distance himself,
as if to say we are merely mortal,
not the gods we thought we were.
St. Stephen seems to have abandoned
his flock, bolted his doors and gone to ground.
Between the heavy, heaving gravestones
daffodils are nodding and bending
their heads in sympathy, I see,
as if to remind us that our longing
for immortality remains.

Up the slope and here's the canal,
flat as a mirror of pure light, rippled
only by the slow paddling of coots
and moorhens innocently mingling.
Down the slope and Mr Heath, I know,
will be fresh from his own safe bed,
fleeced and walking his dalmatian.
Self-consciously we will curve
away to the recommended distance,
smile to each other knowingly
and raise our eyebrows as we pass.
Round the corner, the pearly gates
of the Co-op are waiting for all of us.

## In praise of trees?

We are too sentimental about trees.
Roof tiles are lifting and rattling, leaves
thrashing against my attic window
as if in anger with the bristling air.
They live and breathe and, for all I know,
may love and be holding subterranean hands
with other plane trees along the road.

But they grow muscular and dangerous
and do not need our eulogies or reverence.
In towns, parched and choking,
heavy with spring,
they will happily stove in a roof
or a bus if their thirsty gods decree it.
Like us they clamber up and over each other
to demand the sunlight, their share of rain.

Chopped or burned, with hardwood hearts
and certainty, they scatter their future,
leave filaments of roots dormant
under sand, hibernating under concrete.
They understand a tipping point,
will know when we have reached it.

## Of weeds.....

Forty nine, she found, down one suburban road,
has labelled, sketched and painted them.
How can anyone be passionate, so keen
to identify green things called deadnettle....
milk thistle....polypody....nipplewort?
She loves and rejoices in their names.
All language is a form of labelling,
and there is mythology and a solid body
of evidence behind their lore: as taste,
as cure, as an aid to romance. Imagine
the silk of their skin on your hands,
their flesh on your fingers, the sex appeal
of Burdock, Nutsedge, Buckhorn....

## ....and locomotives

Their makers, with their steel and flames
and hammers and raw hands, loved them.
They numbered them but, not content,
endowed them with names and an identity.
And such names! 45604 Ceylon...
45561 Saskatchewan......The Duchess
of Montrose...Aden...Achilles...
Seahorse..Jervis...Mars…
Feel the sound and taste on your tongue,
the history, the echoes, the learning.
They loved the engineering: those tall wheels,
the gearing, the beat of pistons running
like sewing machines, such soft steam.
And, oh! the elegant waist
of a tapering boiler. Alive. Romantic.

## Coming and going

Two women, returning from a conference,
like noisy neighbours share their noisy lives.
They have discussed the chairman, sausages,
bicycles, the chairman, the River Trent,
the price of bread, the chairman.....
In the slow silences one plays with her scarf
and picks at her sandwiches. The other rootles
in her bag for lipstick, tissues, a bag of nuts.

Through the window, station names flash
past like nervous tics too quick to catch.
The lady next to me is on her way to Glasgow,
chattering at first as if she's won the lottery.
Now she sits as still as an hour hand, her head
deep in in a novel while her narrative flies by.
A suited man, his frown illuminated, is sending
love and sales figures at the speed of light.

The door slides open….closed…slides open….
Time and our feelings, it seems, are relative.
Outside, distant hills lie sound asleep,
fields with dots of sheep are rolling along,
barns with mouths wide open in amazement
offer a glimpse of tractors like tonsils.
Lines of tired pylons, legs bending
under their own weight, are strolling home.

## The Violent Land

Think of all the poets who wake at 10 past 5
before it's light, driven by the birth pangs
of a big idea or a word or phrase,
who fumble for their pen and note pad,
an abandoned scrap of paper perhaps.
Or, if you're desperate like me, the back
of an old cowboy book, a library discard
called 'The Violent Land'.

While poets lie there musing and dozing,
their ears opening and closing
to the sound of the early birds and pigeons,
the man sneezing in the room next door,
the hero is in his saddle before the sun is up.

Jed Stone, a rancher and a man of few words,
is struggling in the wilderness
to forge a life of peace amongst the guns.
This is a copy of the poem I scribbled
and left unpolished for him in the back of the book.
It seemed the least I could do.
There wasn't much poetry around
in Oregon, in those days.

## Just not p.c. to say it

It was the Yankees baseball cap, the jeans
and white trainers that gave it away.
A youth who doesn't understand boundaries
trying to set his own — trying it on,
managing to look both shifty and brazen.
I try not to judge, make assumptions.
This is public transport after all, so
you have to mingle with the great unwashed.

Time was, though, you knew
First Class meant respectable; smart suits
and ties, men of money and business.
I've paid a premium for wi-fi and space,
clean antimacassars and a bit of peace.
It's just dishonest. I shouldn't be made
to feel like joining the Ticket Police.

I want to turn vigilante, tell him
'It's a form of theft. You are a thief,
wanting something for nothing.'
Someone has to set the standards,
teach respect for the system, the rules.
Otherwise we all lose, go down
the long slide into anarchy.

But I don't. I just look at him in a knowing
'I've got your number' kind of way.
I tell myself, 'Let it go. Leave it
to the ticket inspector, if he ever appears.
It's not my job. It's his.
Tell him out loud for all to hear,
including the youth,
that you don't want to perch on seats
where people have put their feet up,
depositing dog-shit or bubblegum
from their shoes onto your trousers.'

## Amsterdam

I expected Rembrandt at every turn.
What I found was bicycles – stampedes
of shining handlebars like Longhorns
corralled in herds by day, docile and tethered
in long racks, their sturdy steel frames
and front wheels rearing up, waiting
for the time when they are free to run again
along spaghetti-like, dedicated lanes.

No Lycra here, or helmets; no carbon frames
harnessed by figures hunched over front forks,
feet punching the air into submission behind them,
chins determined to streamline themselves.
Just T shirts and jumpers, jackets and suits
passing each other gently, weaving alongside
still canals, over cobbles and under plane trees.

All sitting up and begging, straight-backed,
their knees and calves rising and falling
like miniature beam engines pivoting,
propelling them in a fluid forward motion.
And pedals whirring in perfect circles, combining
easy speed with freedom and freewheeling.

They are streetwise, these bikes; modest beings
wearing sky blue tyres to celebrate city life,
their chains chuckling and whispering;
their saddles sitting over clacking mudguards
bearing panniers for paints and bobble hats,
flat luggage racks for toddlers and books,
baskets for fruit and veg or a cute family pooch.

They come alive when out of doors, when
the rain could be a drowning or a sweet relief,
the wind an unpredictable resistance or a friend;
so that cycles and cyclists are one, joined at the hip
in a joy of mutual love and respect.
And best of all, in this union of souls
the riders' heads are up, their eyes engaged
with the lost and dying art of looking around.

## Pistol

Your damp palms might hold me firm,
your fat fingers gently squeeze
as you close one eye.
But I am the one — the bringer of death.
I am the one who explodes inside,
feels the flame, the acid heat
like a deadly attack of heartburn
my liver and spleen must cope with.
I smell the acrid smoke in my nostrils.

You see, I am made in your own image.
My spontaneous combustion
projects a high-speed missile,
a baby I have carried and cradled,
its spirals spinning, diminishing
until it is merely a speck in the air.

My eyesight is perfect. Spot on, you might say.
I see it shoot away, plunge into the target.
I feel the heartbeat of a deer as it reels
back and blacks out, feel the spurt of blood
from a man's chest as he hits the deck.

**Agenda**

Overnight the village has been bombed
by silent aircraft from the oest.
There are no tanks outside the Co-op
but collateral damage is widespread.
Mrs Jones, out walking her labradoodle,
has found trees wearing knitted bow ties,
railings sporting multi-coloured mittens,
lights adorned with bobble hats in pink
like so much woolly shrapnel,
as if the gods of war had decided
to pull their party poppers.

If only all invasions could be such fun,
cast on in gardens over tea and buns.
born out of a cultural agenda of the womb.
I wonder where our warriors have gone,
men of steel prepared to test themselves.
We seem to care about the Middle East,
the ice pack, the fate of Villa or United,
but in an isolated, non-committee sort of way.
We have forgotten how to be loud,
tinkering behind our garage doors,
drumming quietly in the shed
at the bottom of the garden.

## Peppa Pig

Though all is changed and cheap
I am surprised. You must admire its confidence:
the new curved lines of shelves, arcs of spines,
random angles and the bending space between,
the leaf-and-soil decor of bark and green.

But words still define and shape these things.
That hide-bound dusty silence may have gone
but you can hear how the page still sings;
can pause at a title that catches your eye,
linger a while and open its wings.

Enter with a ready heart and open mind.
Dock your iPod, flick on the machines,
love and light up the faces of screens, learn
to 3-D print a model of a stranger's face
and scroll the rolling web from page to page.

In here is still the best and worst of everything;
all that we are, and with imagination yet might be.
I found Creation bound by a theory of string,
little Peter Rabbit talking loudly to Odysseus,
Peppa Pig talking proudly to Pythagoras.

## ...Action

Boxing Day, and I'm in the hotel library slumped
in front of the fire with a book on my lap,
dozing between chapters of *The Red Queen*
which had caught my eye on the shelf
like a pound coin spotted on the pavement.
I must look like an actor learning his lines.

At the far end two glass doors arch
like clear church windows, and through them
I can see a black and white print of a sheep dog
who seems to be smiling at something.
Waiters in black shirts and long black aprons
are crisscrossing in front of him,
like jackdaws acting in a Feydeau farce
or stage hands changing the set between acts.

As if on cue, enter stage right two breasts
in a red jumper, as shocking
as a random daub in a Turner painting.
They peer into the library and their owner,
not seeing who she wants, spins on her right heel,
flicks her left leg up and behind as if practising
the quickstep with a partner in the wings,
then slips off stage right, leaving behind
the sheep dog, with his smile broadening.

## **Skara Brae** *

*after George Mackay Brown*

Long before the dawn, the long dawning,
before the iron,
they worked STONE with stone tools,

quarried monoliths,
inched them using miles of bladder wrack.

Here, at the edge of the world, they engineered:
erected shrines to the liminal
in heaving circles.

They understood the power of SUN,
built burial mounds
the shape of loaves to mirror
the rise of their constant hills.

This was a special place, a hub.
Here they taught their bairns syllables
for DEATH and BLOOD and BONE,

moved beyond the slow wisdom
of stone into the crucible of WORDS,
laid neural pathways down generations
to lift us out of darkness,

opened up our minds like swans' wings,
like bell heather to the LIGHT.

## Fradley Airfield

First light guides us in. The air thrums.
Dusty vans taxi like memories of Spitfires
past high ranks of pallets.
Heavy artics trundle like Lancasters
out of half-moon hangars, rumble
down the runways with their payload.
Inside, we handle lettuces as gently as bombs.
We're the lucky ones. The ghosts
of all the young who bit their thumbs
at death haunt our long-lived lives.

**Settlement**

We came from the sea to kill
with sword and axe,
risked the riptides, rose
out of a haar
as white as a dragon's breath
and stumbled across these outcrops

where Sea and Rock
have come to mirror each other
in the wave-swell of fields,
in these rolling hills contoured
like humpbacked whales.

We named them Orknayjar,
the islands of seals.
Perch on the cliff's edge,
look down the gully where Water
has chiseled an entrance
like the eye of a needle,
where the sea tries to thread herself.

Her wind-tormented skin is unrelenting
in its liquid motion, and today she spits
and hurls herself
against the rock's solidity,
its damned immovability.

We stood then at the edge of a world
where Rock slips
below the waves
like a drowning man,
crossed a causeway at low tide
and climbed to the steep drop,

found for the first time
that sense of separateness,
the safety
that comes with islands

where everyone is known
and distant lords rule with leniency.

## Bridges

This is my uncle Albert — all ginger hair
and ears like saucers, that cheeky smile
as if he's pinched the last chocolate biscuit.
'Not a bad bone in his body,' I'm told.
'Wouldn't hurt a fly.' This was before the war,
before the children he would never have.

Killed he was, parachuting in at Arnhem.
A bridge too far for him, he came down
with a hole in his back the size of my fist.
This photo was taken outside the mill gates
on Crimea street. Nineteen he was. A hero.
I bear his name and carry it with pride.

My oldest daughter's settled now, at home
with the kids, with the steep green hill
and dots of sheep behind. She has his smile,
that hint of mischief. And that ginger hair
that's crossed a generation.
In the end some bridges build themselves.

**And so…**

It’s after lunch and we’re on the sofa chatting.
Catching the whispers, he asks, ‘Is Auntie Cath
having a baby?’ So mum explains it is the size
of a strawberry just now and growing, just as he is.

Minutes later he returns, says nothing, but
with unedited feeling and feather-like
gentleness strokes her tummy, and skips out.
He is amazing himself, and so is readily amazed.
And isn't that the truth of things.

Later his younger sister saunters in, says nothing,
cuddles up to Auntie Cath, and with unscripted delicacy
kisses her tummy and skips out.
She is so loving herself, and so is easy to love.
And isn’t that the truth of things.

## Miracle

How did this come about, the two of us,
swaddled in this shaded room?
I have counted twenty ticking minutes
since your thumb and you slipped into sleep,
nestled in the bending of my arm,
your warm head heavy on my chest,
your stertorous breath relaxing
with the little in-out rhythm of your heart.
How did I light upon this second coming,
stumbling through the inexorable years
with neither map nor star? I do not know.
I should encourage you to stir,
but we shall tarry — you, wherever you are,
me, with my breath feathering your hair.

**Boy**

He is remarkable. He talks and talks,
and talks and tells, and talks and asks.
He asks about superheroes, how eagles fly,
why two and two make four, not six.
He wonders how to ride a bike with one-hand,
why his sister likes to be a pink princess
rather than the pilot of a spacecraft.
His bedroom is a battlefield of tranklements
among a thousand Lego bits he finds a use for.

He inhabits a private place of great discoveries
and territories needing to be mapped,
of words like a fluttering of startled birds,
a multi-coloured cascade of smarties.
He is busy making sense of life as it happens,
learning about body and soul, how it feels
to be alone, to show affection, to break a bone.

To him it must seem like a puzzle to be solved,
a jigsaw in need of constant re-arrangement,
a restlessness surging through him
like the coming and going of bees to their hive.
To spend a day with him is joyful, witnessing
the working of those tiny sparks of lightning,
this miracle made vocal, until he falls asleep
so peacefully you can hardly hear him breathing.

## Intensive care

Back from theatre, again, the room quiet
but for your breathing and the syllables
of monitors and voices in the corridor,
your eyes closed in opiate delirium
you whispered, 'I'm being chased
around the room by a mashed potato.'
And, after a silence, 'Is that you, dad?'
and you squeezed my hand.

To see your pale flesh turn red and swell,
a doctor's pen daily marking out the fronts,
was to witness life reduced
to mortal combat between microbes.
If only love could be a friendly bacteria
we could drip-feed into veins.
But for now at least, thank God for surgeons
and men of science, and Fleming.

And yes, thank God for love.
Had you gone before your time, the natural
order disturbed, I would have needed
your absence, the silences, made bearable;
convinced myself you were still somewhere:
in the low clouds, your voice in the wind,
your hands part of the warm rain.
Heaven would be good. That's what it's for.

## Off

Imagine the pent-up energy,
the violence, of a single electron
spinning madly around its nucleus,
unable to break free, millions of them
going nowhere in the red-hot cauldron
of their universe.

Until some outside force charges in
and scatters them, or marches them in lines,
directing them to travel North or South.
Imagine their excitement at the thought
of having somewhere to go.

There are such moments, when the world shifts.
Imagine Einstein pushing off his little boat
at midnight across a sea of relativity —
all those ricocheting atoms.
Or Rutherford as he fired his first alpha particles.
All those electrons suddenly weighing up
the possibilities, high-fiving, punching the air.

## Fault-line

It is easy to be jealous of the young;
difficult to face the onslaught
of their certainty, their stamina,
their bounce on the dance floor
while we're reduced to a few stiff 'moves',
as self-conscious as burglars.

I know it has always been so.
Old men toil in the fields while the young
go off to war singing, bearing the brunt
of ideas more powerful than kings and bombs,
carrying the burden of bad choices.

We have left them only toys,
to download lives that fit into a pocket,
to scroll a kind of meaning out of emptiness
while the tiny spheres of their lives contract
like stars preparing to implode.

It takes a tragedy to make a generation unlearn.
Now they have lives that slide beneath them:
can never power down the drip of data.
This tap-dance is their inheritance.
I fear for them. The way they understand
so little, know so much.

## Fighting talk

It was the year Man first took a walk
in space and our Earth became
a small blue marble in the black void.
And so we essayed in Marx and Mao
and tutored ourselves in love and peace.
And in November the deep snow came,
solidified, and stayed.

That winter a bus slid backwards down a hill,
marble washstands froze
and snowmen lost their innocence,
and when the wind blew in from the Urals
it was Arctic with subversion.
We were all snowmen then,
when spies came in from the cold
and contaminated snow cruised down,
dendrites thick as a nuclear arsenal.

And our flowers grew militant.
We found our voice by sitting in,
by marching on silos at missile sites,
by hurling cobblestones down boulevards.
All things seemed possible.
We clamoured for new politics, fresh starts,
and with our older bones and in our hearts
we are still here, still clamouring.

## In the moment

They stand dotted about, still as stalagmites,
waiting. 'Jayne is wonderful,' they tell me.
They do what they can, one or two from chairs,
with legs and arms and stout hearts.

Warmed up, they pull out of the earth
invisible strings, imagine heavy heads to be balloons.
When the music comes in quietly, like a friend,
hips sway and arms swing with easy rhythm.
They balance as they have always done
with their spouses and the choices made,

and they are dancing round their handbags,
arms and wrists bending and weaving
into a hand jive, into the teamwork of The Routine
Best of all, the men have joined them on the dance floor.

Suddenly they are all pointing upwards, left and right,
as if to signal their future in the stars,
for all the world like Go-Go Dancers
wagging their fingers at arthritis and life's vicissitudes.
They clap in unison, stretch like Adam
reaching for the apple, lift like mist the weight
of the world from their shoulders.

They dance like gentle clubbers, with nothing to prove,
each movement a testament to life.
In the moment, their bodies are all they know.
Being alive is their baseline, empathy their bedfellow.
They share experience, the wisdom from giving birth
and rearing, and letting go, and loss.

Tears buried deep, difficult to move as wisdom teeth
for some, come easily to others
and coffee time is biscuit sweet with friendship.
Their creed is to accept.
They laugh aloud at stories, at the memory,
the mention, of heavy breathing.

## Being

*eventually all things merge...*
*...and a river runs through it. (Norman Maclean)*

They are waiting
for something to happen,
have settled on the bank behind,
their legs stretched out, intrigued
by the way I am weaving the rod in the air
and the line unrolling like spun sugar
before relaxing on the water.

They ask me why I do it.
I try to explain, describing
an underwater universe of plants
and snails and nymphs.
How trout are carnivores
and eat to survive; how they rush
to the surface to gobble up a mayfly,
a moth or a daddy-long-legs.

I try to explain the dance
and rhythm of a rolling cast,
the day-long cocoon of anticipation.
That it isn't really about the catching
or taking of a fish, reeling it in
as you might a kitten
tugging on a ball of string.

It’s the sky, the running home of the river,
being at one with the swan and the damselfly,
being other, being out of yourself.
They nod, look blank and stroll on.
To them it must appear as pointless
as chasing a cheese downhill
or growing alfalfa.

## Camus explains football to his second wife

Over the onion soup, playing idly
with his cubes of croutons, he is musing
about life and the importance of football.
'Ma chère,' he says, 'everything I know
of value, of morality and obligation,
I owe to football.

You have menstruation and childbirth,
a home to give you meaning... a purpose,
but I need the passion of football
...as much as my mistresses.
It is life beyond the home and insignificance.
It is a physical struggle for more'.

On his napkin he draws her a picture of two
players frozen in mid-dance, and tells her
that when he pirouettes around the ball
or executes a pas de deux with a team mate
it is a source of pride and joy and self-esteem.
'And for that moment my soul is lifted.

It is a theatre,' he says, 'where the cast,
in the struggle for victory together,
create their own meaning....by refusing
to be merely what they are.
And the anticipation of the next pass,
the next chip and flick and body swerve
— those moments, are the only future.'

Over the soufflé he falls into a reverie.
'When a man controls the ball he is the sun
choreographing the universe,
as if it were his destiny. And he is saying,
*I'm here! I matter. I make a difference,*
*in a world where nothing really matters.*

But I understand... the idea is patently absurd.
If the game goes badly and we lose, then I lose.
Am I then alone? What would you have me do?
Kill myself, or have a beer?'

And then he pauses, and says, 'If we knew
why we exist, football would not exist.
It is a metaphor...for the point of it all,
like the moment you hold your child
for the first time'.

## X marks the spot

You may remember those long-defunct,
inky Green or Pink local newspapers.
They featured a weekly treasure map,
an island of grey faces and flat caps
forming a background like foggy weather
to an action picture of Brylcreemed men
in long shorts and baggy shirts: acting
as landmarks to a missing ball that promised
wealth, and a brighter future doing nothing.

The ball was never where you thought
from the players' contorted postures: usually
a keeper high in the air, his arms extended
and fists like hams trying to punch it away,
with an opponent leaping as if jumping over
hot coals to get there with his head.
Often a defender stood rooted to the spot
as if his studs were stuck in the mud.

Knowing the odds I would put my X's
tightly clumped together in a small square
where logic said it shouldn't be.
Then, out of the pink, I won £100 — a fortune.
I'm still not sure how this happened,
but the cheque seemed to slip into the coffers
of some random jewelers in Bolton to pay
for a sapphire and gold engagement ring.

Three grandchildren and a lifetime later
that X still marks the spot on your finger.
I'd like to think it was good judgement, not luck,
but either way some prizes are worth winning.

## Holidays

used to happen
somewhere special, an escape.

Not everywhere so nowhere.
Not up green mountains,
down white slopes, on beaches,
on trains and slow boats,
in posh galleries and bars,
in cottages surrounded by cows.

I used to happen.
Someone special, escaping.

A boy with a quiff on a tram,
a father with a dream and a pram,
a balding ape with his toes in the sand.
Not everywhere so nowhere.
Not this pear-shaped figure
stalking me in shop windows,
in bathrooms.

## Castelsardo

Sardinia. A blue and blinding sky, the air
an oven, the barrel-vaulted nave an escape.
Before the marbled altar two rows of bent
backs beneath black headscarves, the poor
women of this bleached and ancient town,
elderly yet kneeling in prayer, recited
their Gregorian chant like a murmuration
in Latin — smooth and gliding, repeated
in unison, over and over, again and again,
on and on: solemn, steady and insistent.

Within this sacred, stone space of sound
these sunbaked, toughened grandmothers
surrendered themselves to the rhythm
of their Gregorian chant — hypnotised
into an altered state of mind, soothed
by a letting go and lifting into a sanctuary
of peace, a purging of the bruising
to their bodies and souls. A blessing,
like a strong drug or medicine, that only God
and heaven it seems can provide for them.

**Haibun**

Cherish your name. It holds the weight of love given as a gift by your parents. It is the sound of a new-born infant, a child safe in a soft bed, the squeal of playtime. Now it is the silence of absence, the sound of generations calling across the water

> the distant cry of my dreams
> when the nights are winter-long
> and the sea sits quietly.

She remains elusive, the friendly lady — a shape without substance, with her string of old men visiting each afternoon in smart suits, her curtains closed like silent messages. She was a suggestion, a hint of excitement still to be discovered. With hindsight I wonder what her quiet neighbours, in their speech bubbles behind shut doors, thought. And how much they heard.

> Silk robe, satin skin, yields,
> used, abused, always adored
> in an urgent way.

## Set in my ways

It is shocking to see. Gaggles of girls
out on the lash at chucking out time,
on heels like spikes or tower blocks,
with red exaggerated lips as ripe as plums,
stumbling and flaunting their cleavage
and bare midriff, flashing their thighs
in winter.

Young women have always teased, dressed
like hymns to all things bright and beautiful,
each a work of art of the colourist school
and accessorized to emphasise their sex.
Being themselves, without charm or shame.
Girls do want a good time, I know.
It isn't new.

Debs 'came out', all lipstick and ball gown,
long gloves and cigarette holders.
They screamed for Rolling Stones and Beatles.
But now it's middle-aged singletons,
and their mums, letting their hair down literally
at hen parties in Glasgow or Dubrovnik.

## Scar

I was eight, too gentle and too young
for anger and retaliation.
Streetwise, at ten, his crew cut greased
and sharp as a hedgehog, he told me
to walk round two sides of a triangle
of scrub while he cut across the base.
He was waiting, and laughing,
his mouth as wide as a tunnel
with that mocking sound of triumph.

Clearly he understood triangles
and the naivety of smaller boys,
and at that moment my inner self split
open like a fallen chestnut.

Sixty years, and I'm still on that corner,
wondering whether he's still alive,
whether he still takes advantage of the gentle
as he cuts imagined enemies down to size,
whether he has inherited the Earth.
Or whether there has been a retribution,
some clipping of wings and claws,
the balancing which Mother Nature loves.

## A history of pets

Well, it started with the tortoise, tethered
to a drainpipe in the yard, its leather neck
exposed and jabbing in and out, grabbing
bits of lettuce and nibbling his string.
Each dash for freedom we would find it
buried in the coal shed, a black shell
shining like a kneecap. Pointless…
stolen by the soot-faced coalman.

And then the mongrel chased its drooping tail
all day, clockwise like a whirling dervish,
his mouth and face in a distorted grin.
I kept my hands behind my back
well clear of his yellow teeth.
His yowling and barking at something
I couldn't see cracked the air, fractured
the front room, the kitchen, the stairs.
Ran away overnight, they said.

A child can't love a real-life monster.
Even the budgie would thrash its wings
like a blue archangel skimming my head,
me ducking like a nervous pilot in a dogfight.
It wreaked havoc in the small front room,
crashing into the windows and walls,
its radar gone, until it broke its neck.
A jolt, a snap, and suddenly a dead body.
We buried it in a brown paper bag.

And then two goldfish, following some
anti-clockwise instinct around a plastic frond
became transparent, much too visceral,
their swim bladders swollen and disturbing.
In the end we watched them flush away,
circling the pan like scraps of paper.
Swimming their way to the sea, they said.

I have no children. Don't feel the need.
I keep no pets, can't stand the littering,
the odour of dog's bodies on the cushions,
the noise, the flutter and fleas of them.
I keep a wife – she is obedient, well trained,
well fed. She is still here.

## Scary

Help! I'm being followed, haunted
by a stranger like a spirit from the other side,
like a third-rate private detective
without the black-and-white fedora,
or a magician — *Now you see me, now you don't.*
Sometimes I spot him in shop windows
shambling along as if he has a gammy knee,
as if in mockery, as a child would.

I see him in the pub, behind the bar
raising a pint in sardonic greeting,
his bald dome shining in the downlights.
I turn away, flick my eyes back to catch him out
but there's no escape. It's impossible to grasp
a ghost as elusive as a round-shouldered shadow
behind me on a sunny afternoon.

In the bathroom, where he gets too close,
he holds up hands like pork chops
to examine red blotches, the rifts in his skin,
pokes at bags like loofahs under his eyes.
He dares me to stare him out, but whether
he is threatening or beckoning, I don't know.
It's as if he wants to be friends.
Part of me thinks I should reach out,
get to know him better, see what he wants.

## Just now and then

Thirteen is the number of times, I'm told,
a normal cell can reproduce itself.
So the heart is bound to harden, or soften.
And when love shrinks, lust is lost
and passion comes less often.
Intensity will most likely come
from sudden sickness, or a gun.
Sometimes we manufacture it, suck
a lemon during sex, dare ourselves to run
for a bus or jump over a low wall.
Sometimes a poem will bring a little 'Yes!'
catching Time in a yew, or a tight dress,
reminding us it's all still in there,
buried in the rubble, somewhere.

## The mortality of socks

*with thanks to Arnold Bennett*

He was an inconsistent man, difficult
to fathom and hard to love.
The sort of man who would buy six
blue suits together, but hated
the mortality of socks, resented
the expense when one wore out.

I see myself in him. Socks matter.
I would answer the door naked
as long as I had my socks on, although
sex with your socks on is clearly a no-no.

Like him, I do like to be sock-rich.
I open my drawer and enjoy the sight
of rainbow rows of them like sets of twins,
and I save the orphans
until a matching one comes along.

But why do I get a potato in one heel,
or one random toe peeping out like a burglar?
It's a mystery. It's not as if I have one leg,
or a limp, or I hop about a lot.

I like plain blue socks for black shoes
and happy ones with fat green stripes,
or post office red that make a statement.
After all, people pay attention to your socks.

Sometimes I choose to wear odd ones
just to seem a touch eccentric.
But I do wonder.
If a man wears bright yellow does he lack taste?
Can you tell an honest politician from his socks?

## Garden

I think I understand a garden: the fact of it.
A palette of reds and pinks, the bruise
of grape hyacinth; a canvas of green
with copper shrubs, the rain-soaked shed
tucked away. The Feng Shui of it.

And you, out there playing God:
pruning, dead-heading geraniums,
re-seeding and potting out sweet peas ,
your hands digging in and sifting soil,
or cutting relentless grass.

But I cannot find affection for a daffodil
or pause to wonder at a crocus,
or delight in a rose that smells of soap.
I cannot feel cross with a slug
surviving in a thicket of small things.

God might have been a gardener
but he's up there with binoculars,
eyes trained on huge patches of trees,
long ranges of peaks, the blue horizon.
The big picture is his.

And if you feel in your bones
the swell and the call of the sea, the pull
of geology — the weight and the thrust of rock
and the height and the winds of it,
then a garden is just not enough.

## Sea

I saw myself today, at the sea's edge
(as it must be at the end when you float
above and see your body prone
on clean white sheets),
his sandals abandoned by the distant dunes,
a bald head hot as a skillet shining in the sun,
long white ribs ridged like ladders
of razor clams, two hairless knees
lumped like oyster shells.

Here was a creature shedding his skin
for a fortnight, gazing over the water,
the trail of his feet imprinting the sand.
He stood so still, a flotsam of bi-ped
looking up at the sky, the waves bathing
his feet tempting him, calling us home.

**Just possibly…**

There are such moments.
When the disc of the sun became a ball.
When a single Homo erectus slipped
off a fallen log and realised the wheel.
When with a single image, an event horizon*,
we have witnessed, like the disciples
before us, the glow of a future.

We have seen that light can curve,
seen it arcing like a miracle down
into the black vacuum of a beyond that devours all,
sucks secrets forever into oblivion.
This singularity opened up to our imagination
a possibility, a place where time
as we know it stops and some greater force
keeps all in balance.

Beautiful. In this the year of our Lord
we may have seen eternity made manifest.
It has nestled now in our minds like a white dove.
And I have felt in my ready heart for the first time
the great Mystery imagined, in faith
and with hope, by scientist and priest alike.

**the ring of bright light around a black hole*

## From an Orkney window

The Autumn equinox, and the weather
has turned petulant and moody.
A dark pall is lowering over
the black and brooding humps of Hoy
where Pluto is waiting at the gates
of Hades. He is angry.

Yesterday the wind was howling,
rattling barn doors, hissing and spitting,
insinuating itself into every crack and hinge
like a warning.
Beneath the window a quilt of barley
was rippling and flattening itself one minute,
stirring and wrestling with itself the next
in gusts of torment,
as if the crust of the earth beneath
was shuddering.

Today the sky is blue and silent
above the flat circumference of fields,
as if Ceres overnight has accepted her loss.
It is judgement day.
The farmer is out there early, inspecting
his crop, pinching seed-heads
between finger and thumb.
Today we will see the threshing machine.
A plague of geese has settled
by the cool trout-filled loch, honking
as if they know.
This last harvest of the year
will bring them the feast
of the fallen seeds.

**At St. Winnow Church, Cornwall**

Autumn, and I have come again to rest a while and dwell
upon St Winnow's wind-worn stone, its steep and wooded
isolation, the river's tidal rise and fall.
To draw comfort from this sense of permanence.

If a crematorium can feel like a full stop, this graveyard is a pause.
So rest in peace,

**William Saul**
**Buried 16th day of februarie**
**in the year of our Lord God 1651.**

St. Winnow's bells still ring out your name across the estuary
of centuries.

And, if gravestones bear the heavy weight of loss
it is their sad text that brings the lightness of permanence.
Here lies such grief that we must chisel out our own eternity
and carve the names of our young like runes.

**In memory of three beloved grand-children.**
**John.**
**Who died July 20th 1851, aged 10 years.**
**Gertrude.**
**Who died Nov. 15th, 1853, aged 15 months.**

**And Helen Gertrude.**
**Who died March 16th, 1855, aged 8 months.**

So young,

but these bells will ring out their names across the centuries. St. Winnow understood what we too easily forget, that faith holds hands across the generations.

See, here:

**IN**
**LOVING MEMORY**
**OF**
**a son**
**Who died 11th May 1944**
**aged 17 days.**

**SLEEP WELL, LITTLE MAN**

**Acknowledgements**

'Blackbird' was featured in *The Northampton Poetry Review*

'Off' won the 2017 *Poetry on Loan* competition.

'Claymills Pumping Station' featured in *The Poetry of Staffordshire* from Offa's Press.

'Haibun' featured in *Ripening Cherries* from Offa's Press.

'They thought us beautiful' and 'Pistol' featured in the pamphlet *Mapography* published by the Brampton Gallery and Museum.

'Miracle' was shortlisted in the Poetry on Loan competition in 2020, under the title 'Counting'.

My grateful thanks go to Roger Elkin for his invaluable advice in the 'making' of this collection, and to those poetry friends who have offered considered thought about many of the poems.

## About Bert Flitcroft

Bert Flitcroft was born and brought up in Lancashire but now lives in the Midlands. He has two collections of poetry published: *Singing Puccini at the Kitchen Sink* and *Thought-Apples*. His work has appeared in a number of national magazines. He is a prize-winning poet, has been Poet in Residence at the Southwell Poetry Festival and has performed at a number of national festivals including The Edinburgh International Book Festival. He was Staffordshire Poet Laureate 2015–17, and curated the on-line *Staffordshire Poetry Collection.*

He has worked as resident poet with one of our 'National Treasures', The Wedgwood Collection at the V&A; as resident poet with the prestigious R.I.B.A exhibition 'The Road Less Travelled'; and recently as part of the University of Keele project 'Labelling the Museum'.